Variations
on a Theme of Love

poems by

Kathy O'Fallon

Finishing Line Press
Georgetown, Kentucky

Variations
on a Theme of Love

because of the loons
moon reaches into the lake
and pulls him to her

ACKNOWLEDGMENTS

Publisher: Leah Huete de Maines
Editor: Christen Kincaid
Cover Art: Michelangelo: *The Creation of Adam,* Public Domain
Author Photo: Harmony Walton
Cover Design: Elizabeth Maines McCleavy

Order online: www.finishinglinepress.com
also available on amazon.com

Author inquiries and mail orders:
Finishing Line Press
PO Box 1626
Georgetown, Kentucky 40324
USA

Contents

Sunrise and Dogwood: A Reconciliation

The moment when dream-speak bridges
the veil between worlds, and hope is fragile.

When rain's a prayer, and the dogwood
has just begun to flower. When, with the grace

of cloud-break, the sun, with all its cleaving,
must rise. Who else to spotlight my blooming

crabapple, the gabled rooftop next door, bare
branches of twin oaks that touch from both

yards, and over the fence we fought about,
white blossoms, in a wonder of crosses.

What Child Is This

Want
from the womb, to birthing-pool-
warm, swaddle of skin-to-skin
and stream from the nipple, only
the faces of so-happy-to-see-her,
rocking and hum. Wonder of form—
oh yes—and eyes, a new telescope.
Her own breath in the cosmos.

Taste
and smell—mouth's yum-tongue,
milking the mother's pearl, hint
of her pickled dinner, saliva lifeblood,
the sour upchuck. Body not hers—
its salty signature inside out!
And the strange neutrality of cotton,
explosion of menthol massage.

Sleep,
leaving again, weaving the before
and yet-to-come, dreaming
the unknowable preview—muscle
of wings a blue tendril let go
and the reunion of gill-lungs.
What is this running? What
are these legs? To where? Wake up!

Sound
no longer an echo—soprano
of sparrow and thrush, haunting
of loon. Hoot owl. That familiar
rush of water, alto of wind its twin,
quartet of air in color—mauve,
the tinkle of pink, chords of gray,
that almost white-light silence.

Want
and want and want—the clock
dry-faced and ticking, the world
a spinning mobile disappearing,
not yet rage of purple—who is she,
beast or baby—drowning eyes
and grasping limbs, screams. Lies
of lullabies, now and not forever.

Listening for Tchaikovsky

Violin Concerto Op. 35

Sometimes, when his band would get a gig, my dad
would be gone for hours—a wedding or dance
if he was lucky—his lips wet with the spit
of the trumpet's mouthpiece (and who knows what else),
valves oiled, and slides, greased pistons, pipes.
And with his instrument all polished and shiny,
the smooth sounds of Belafonte and the jazz of Louis.
My dad, dimple-chinned, long and lean—Cary Grant,
some thought—man, he could really blow a horn,

but home was where I lived, greedy for evenings
without the slingshot of his tempers, where I could rest
my head to the click of Mom's violin case opening,
the clack of the music stand unfolding, the oily smell
of resin-stroked bow-hairs, knowing what she loved
was tucked under her chin, right elbow cocked
like a wing, ready for take-off, and the sound of Heifetz
leading his flock to *Romeo and Juliet*, where music flew
to the cage of my dreams, safe as unsafe could be.

The Facts of Life

White-blue skies and quiet,
air close enough to wet your upper lip.
We could have been outside roller skating—
two sisters—around and around our dead
end, or shooting cats' eyes on the asphalt
until the heat won. We probably came in
through the basement up the stairs to the hall
past the living room, where we weren't used
to much living going on.

There on the couch: our parents braided
to each other's bodies like a pastry or roll
of Christmas wrap—the way it unravels
when it's pulled. Our mother, a secret
siren, a co-conspirator? Impossible—
a sorcerer's spell! Mermaid transmutation—
her flaming curls like tide-washed kelp,
pearl-drop sweat tearing her freckled face,
and flickers flying from the nest! Back-
stroking a thirsty sea/a roiling river,
her center sinking just enough to disappear.
Did she know she could drown—no,
was drowning?

Dad armed her to the bedroom,
brushed past us like a match.
He could have set the house on fire
for all he paid attention—pyromaniac
oblivious to our concern.
We could have all been consumed.

Out the Church Window One Sunday, Swans

There, across the field, little steepled
churches glide across a heaven too far
to see, brave webbed feet beneath reaching
for the earthly surge of silt and twig
and pollywog, and from the rooftop,
church bells ring, swans announcing union,
rock to feather.

Inside, a preacher drones, a grandpa snores,
heat forms beads of sweat that rain like tears
down dampened faces, wilted children
begging to be freed to bare feet, gleeful
splashing at the water's edge, wedded
to the pond and swans that look like churches,
frogs like gods.

The Dinner Hour

Molding a second skin around
my fingers, I watch the hot wax
drip on the dining room table,
scrape it with an exposed nail
to try and smooth out the finish
so Mom won't notice. The swinging
door from the kitchen slaps open,
her arms laden with a platter of beef.
Sitting to Jimmy's left—by his weak ear,
it turned out—I repeat myself to pass
the peas, the butter, the milk. Jimmy,
the nail on the chalkboard. Like Dad,
who can raise blood from the skin
with his tongue.

I can't catch the wax fast enough.
The table is innocent, the candles,
Mom's artwork—hours of boiling
and shaping mounds of paraffin
for snow around their bases, winding
vines of wax holly with tiny berries
up the tapers. Schlepping back and forth
to wait on her good-for-nothing family,
she throws Dad a look when the yelling
begins, to keep him from carving Jimmy
into little pieces, not that I can lift a finger
to help her, mummified in the warmth
of the wax working its way past my palms.

Thief

If you were blessed to have a mother
in the kitchen not wielding a knife
except to what was already dead,

you might know the feel of saliva
on your tongue, the body in anticipation,
and if you're like me, remember the evil

with which you stole her cookies locked
in the freezer for the neighbors at Christmas,
the melting powdered sugar on the roof

of your mouth like snow, the Hershey's chocolate
a frozen boat of joy sailing you away from your guilt
as if it never existed, while your mother still labored

in the kitchen, grating the parmesan cheese,
pounding the veal, stirring the red sauce
she'd simmer for hours, and you'd scoop

a few spoonfuls when she wasn't watching
until the pot began to look lonely, the kids' food
an afterthought, because special occasions

meant only guests got the fancy, and it didn't
take two hands to count the number of times
their best friends came for dinner and bridge

before you'd left for good, but ice box cake
deserved every kind of stealth for its whipped
cream igloo of wafers, and when you slid the knife

through its chilly foundation, you could hollow out
a room without anyone being the wiser, your gut
the keeper of every wrong move of your help-me-

I-don't-know-what-I'm-doing-childhood,
while you grew and hid deeper by the minute,
though nobody else knew, but isn't that why

the fermenting stink that now simmers
on your stove won't turn sweet?
You will never be as good as your mother.

Love

after Lynn Emanuel

Unlike Jesus in the creche
was I ill-equipped to reach for it,
conceived in a cyclone of seduction,
sucked into its eye with no myth
to catch the fall. *How heel over head
was I hurled dow*n the cold draft
of ambivalence, murmuring a mother's
shame into the confessional of the world.
The shattered lyrics at my feet shone
like jewels. How slippery their surface,
how fresh they smelled. Treasure only
a wise man could discern. And unlike
Jesus who rose in three days from
the dead, my hands kept polishing
and polishing the gold of fools. Love
finds the jeweler hunched over
in the back room of the store,
a loupe to guide her through
the brilliance to the flaws.

Ignorance as Bliss

Before we bought the groceries
or hung our clothes in the closet,
before we screwed
the bed together, or unrolled
the living room rug,
we set up the Yamaha stereo.

He took the left speaker, I took the right—
a sign, I figured—the correct hemispheres
of our brains hooking up. He didn't bother
with directions, but I scoured the Japanese
translations. Each wire from the stereo
to the speakers, the way jumper cables
connect to a car battery—red to red,
black to black? Plug in the wrong wire
and blow the whole system apart, I knew
that much, but indecision meant no music.
Done right, who'd control the sound?
He plugged wires into holes like a surgeon
on steroids. I copied all but the attitude.
Led Zeppelin cranked high and wild.

Agaricales

*the most familiar fungal order of mushrooms, though
difficult to distinguish the harmless from the toxic*

We choose (or does he choose?) to grab the leash
and dog, instead of frolicking in bed,
to investigate the ravages of rain,
the spongy trails, mycelia twined, the gills
engorged, and mushroom volvas formed, of rup-
tured veils where poison can reside. My lover
wanders off, sinks into dying boughs and scrapes
the duff, caresses stipes and caps the way
an angler strokes the rainbows of a trout.
So beauty-drawn—men's curse—he hunts, bewitched
by snowy, velvet touch (Odysseus he is not).
Destroying angels, death and *skull caps* kill.
What will he choose? And will I stay to watch?

How It Is

Always the laundry, a shower, the cleanliness
that keeps you thinking you're a human being.
What to eat, where to get it, how and when.
Remembering prayer, head-nod to all that is.
And work, the daily bread, it too a practice.
Quiet—how to find it, inside the subway,
food court, nightly news, the time you
take us on a road trip, our dog between
a sour silence. Stop at Torrey Pines,
where the surf, its thunder, dunks us
like a baptism. The pull of tides, a chunky
moon, stars to help remind us just how small
we are. And, walking back, feeling lucky—
beloved lab and man and endless shore,
hear no sound—the train around the bend,
and Tanker's thrown so far and fast against
the bluff we can't see where it happened.
Such love, the silence and the roar.

How Love Shows Up

Happy's sleeping at my feet
when the neighbor dog's serenade
woos me from the screen. Bear,
he's called, not for his bass, but
for the brindle. Shaking my head,
I open the door, climb back in bed—
I still can't resist a crooner.
Happy scoots his way to my rear
and Bear sidles up to the headboard,
his butt now within reach,
tells me in his Chewbacca voice
he could use a scratch just above the hip
(an itch that's been plaguing him for weeks).
Happy repositions for a belly massage,
and then the bath begins. His tongue strokes
my arm like a man in heat, works its way up
to the delicious face cream, but what he really
means is: *get your lazy ass out of bed*
for a car ride to the river for a dip.

On our way out, the trash truck,
like a big-bellied Greek charmer,
backs *its* tail up my driveway. I'll love
anyone who relieves me of my garbage.
Off leash at the trail head, the dogs run in
somersaults, and the crows' enthusiasm
at our arrival sounds almost apoplectic—
their upper west-side accent the only
snooty thing about them. An October
breeze anoints from the sky's thurible,
the umbrella of shade—how much Brahma
loved the Buddha. Where one dog sniffs,
the other follows. They take turns peeing
on the Indian paintbrush, greet strangers
on the trail like smoke-signaled kinfolk,
make no exception for the poison oak.

"Fire Only 15% Contained"

Salinas County News Headline, August, 2016

I'm drifting on the clouds of her soprano,
the dips and dives and somersaults,
everything from the Beatles to Deva Premal,
Santa Ynez mountains bursting in the vastness,
packed to the eyeballs for the conference,
from Smart Water to sheer nighties,
CDs stacked, poetry tucked, her wedding ring
absent. From France she carries a wine called *Eden*—
our birthright a musty innocence. I feel myself flush,
her vibratos, the rise and fall of her chest, her breasts,
the Madonna Inn we just passed—bordello bedrooms,
curtains frilly as sonnets—hundreds of miles to the unfamiliar.
Is there a difference between freedom and opportunity?
Highway 1 detours for the firefighters,
the sky hovers thick and colorless.
Dampness gathers like a six-foot swell,
smell of smoke over the Santa Lucias.

The Tor House Beach

She's wearing the purple dress,
the one handed down by her mother

after the cancer when their bodies
could have been twins.

He places his hand on her nape,
traces the curve like a sculptor.

Lavender. Ladder of buttons
from the V in her back to her sacrum,

like tiny, delicate saucers
from a teacup set for dolls.

Emerald twilight swell,
sunset the hues of flamingo.

A squall of sea gulls yearning,
sea lion poised for its meal.

The day behind them, she turns,
cups his chin in her palm,

watches the poem being written,
sea spray misting his skin,

the pulse of the moon pouring
the waves into and over the dunes.

The Golden Gate

for JP 1949-1976—Until 2023 when a net was placed under the Golden Gate Bridge, it averaged thirty suicides a year.

If you were born lucky
your family had a car
and maybe on road trips

you learned to hold your breath
and count on a bridge over water
though you'd run out of   air first

No   I mean if you were born lucky
you had a family
who drove you safely

across water on a bridge
too high and too long
and when it was done

no one laughed
that you'd covered your head
with a blanket   to escape

No   I mean if you were born lucky
you were loved and beautiful
bridges wouldn't tempt you   to jump

Brothers

for Jim

The sun refuses its entrance
but a trickle of mourners file in.
My brother would've complained,
but now's not the time to call him
a whiner, though we used to.
For the family attending, we manage
to sit in birth order. It marks the hole—
no, holes—our father conspicuously
absent living where it doesn't snow,
three sisters religiously boycotting,
our mother in the ether with her son.
A few AAers at the back of the church
I recognize from high school—not much
hair, and ashen. A ridiculous bouquet
of lilies swallows a side table
from another brother's paramour.

Tom heads to the pulpit with a boom box,
tells the story of how his big brother liked
to use his face for exorcisms, contorting
his expression to make the grievers chuckle.
John slinks down at the end of the pew,
and someone behind me stifles a hiccup.
Jim was more tightly wound than most of us,
says my brain to reassure itself. While Tom,
who'd seized the one thing from the clean-up
he was jealous of—Jim's solid body electric
Gibson vintage Les Paul guitar—ends his tale
with Jim's favorite music, The Kinks
"You Really Got Me," or was it "So Tired,
Tired of Waiting." But before the song ends,
the tape player, as if grabbed by a fist, flies
off the edge of the pulpit and breaks.

Santa Anas: Devil Winds

> *"Lore suggests Spanish missionaries detected an evil presence*
> *in the winds....The Portola expedition supposedly encountered*
> *a fierce windstorm on Saint Ann's Day, claiming a saintly rather*
> *than devilish origin."*
>> Nathan Masters, *"Devil Wind: A Brief History of the*
>> *Santa Anas"*

When I was young I must've called him Daddy.
The wind tears limbs from trees too big for whipping,
chimes cry out for rescue—*hide me, don't leave me!*
I search through early black and whites—they scatter—
shut that   window!

The wind tears limbs from trees too big for whipping,
Is Mother here, finally warning, or has he come reminding?
I search through early black and whites—they scatter—
shut that   window!
One picture in a pinafore and Oxfords.

Is Mother here, finally warning, or has he come reminding?
Proof the memory falters, were they always gale-force winds?
One picture in a pinafore and Oxfords,
on his lap and smiling (so was he).

Proof the memory falters, were they always gale-force winds?
Chimney howls the devil, hot and dry the ash-filled plea.
On his lap and smiling (so was he),
When I was very young I called him Daddy.

June Gloom

for Tom

I don't remember much
about the tide, except that
that it was so damned reliable,
shrouding our feet and ankles,
then pulling away for a reprieve.
My brother, a man of silences
against the roar of the moon's pull.
Tall, more Gregory Peck than Cary Grant—
our father's dimpled chin. Del Mar
gets fogged in most Junes, but
that wasn't why he looked so faded.
Chip off the old man's block,
Dad's father would've said,
but what that man didn't know
could have filled an ocean.

Back then seashells still scattered
in the surf. Their broken edges scraped
our brined and wrinkled skin.
I felt shrunk as a yacht on the horizon.
We waded until I'd talked him off
the ledge again, our feet a ghostly purple.
Such a good young man, working hard
not to pull the trigger, and, for decades
after, checked his rage with the safety on.
Until a highway barricade made waste of him.

Poppy Field

acrylic by Mary Brown

Looking at ruin
dropped from their branches
the poppies   like spoiled
cherry tomatoes exposed
to their seeds   or peonies
after a wind   death seems
such a natural thing
matter turns to mulch
becomes itself again

Yes   the forms in all
their wholeness are most
delicious   or crushed
make a lingering perfume
as with a loved one's essence
which memory can return

Think of breatharians
who eat the horizon
for food   Like that
they love and live
dying

Plum

The unassuming plum clothed in earthy
purple, festooned with gray-green velvet.
From the Neolithic—a great survival
instinct. And who can help but notice
its resemblance to a testicle, fertile vessel,
musky as honey, hanging from smooth
but blemished skin—burls and scars
from the trunk's war of growth.

Not since Neruda have I tasted fruit
this juicy, sweet and spunky as a kiss
on a cliff above the surf at St. Tropez.
Mouth sucking magenta, 1812
Overture from the waves, its finale
exploding down my lined and weathered
chin, begging to be licked—yes, violined.
No lover in my midst but my tongue.

Lament of the Golden Hawk

photograph by Dave Woodman

I wanted so much to write an ode
to the golden hawk that faced out
from Dave's birdbath this morning,
head slightly turned toward his camera,
broom tail dipped in the jeweled water,
the magnificence of its feathers soft as
Gabriel's, dressed like a royal in gold
regalia, but the red of its eye warned
of the stretch and rise that can swoop
down and snatch whatever catches
its fancy—like a camera strap hanging
from this silver-haired guy with eyes
the lightest sapphire—snapping Dave's
neck back, the bird squealing in triumph.
An ode to immortalize a beating heart's
rapid-fire that is its nature? Then again,
I've loved this man whose heart I broke
when we were kids, and now he'll never
love me back.

Olympiad in Training

No one watching but maybe
a lifeguard, a passerby searching
for an empty lane, and me, crippled
by the defects of age, doing a modified
doggy paddle, while a young man
torpedoes from one end of the pool
to the other. I give up pretending
not to gawp, switch to a side stroke
for a better angle. This man no mortal,
but Poseidon rising to the surface,
the weight of water like a cloak
thrown off with Herculean strength.
Like Adonis, too, face painted
in zinc, eyes hidden like the sculpture.
His arms' rotation, Moses parting
the sea, thrusting forward against
the underworld. The arch of his biceps
aglow with victories recorded in ink.
Chiseled stone like I'd once touched
in Florence, another David. I can hardly
keep my hands to myself. God, beauty
breaks me quicker than love.

Ode to What Goes Round

When Eratosthenes discovered our planet was round,
captains sailed on under no moon nights and mothers
relaxed their infant-grips, safe from the edge
to the net of the earth, safe from the infinite sky.

Lately everywhere I look I find circles
            it's dizzying   really
so many worlds inside worlds
            our primate heads   each tiny cell
surrounded by the dead in their new wombs
orbs following loved ones like suitors
            the word *poem*   how its vowels swaddle
            fruit hanging like bosoms
in primary colors   bosoms and their testicle buddies
            smoke rings and daisies
            bubbles rising from the firmament
            each tree trunk an elegant circumference
unjaggéd Mother   tubes of a wave   tunnels and caves
            mouths open for laughing   for tongue
kisses   for spinning to the swing   little beads
of passion-sweat   dilated pupils   the *Oh* of orgasm
            dark opening of creation

Gratitude

that the clap of closing shutters
        and crickets warning from the floorboards
are no more than crows' spooky stories
        and small stings for the price of honey

that space is not really space but
        grain after grain after grain
and merged with the updraft of flying
        ash from the dead will never be lonely

that a strawberry moon can guide with its light
        and twin its image on the ocean
though color's just a vivid reflection
        and pink doesn't exist in the spectrum

that by circling the footprints of sandpipers
        peace signs can be viewed from the heavens
and beachgoers can feel some comfort
        along with the humble hermit crab

that the aphrodisiac of the ocean's perfume
        can lift the veil of amnesia
and make me homesick
        for my amphibian

To November

You were once just holiday anticipation
and Saturdays at the stables. All shovel
and spit, I was the fetid sweat of puberty.
Lake Surprise and miles of trails, the grit-
grey of stolen land, Watchung's. Perfume
of wealth in leather tack, paddock boots,
upholstery. Earth-brine from the stalls—
the smelling salts of urine, with dung-steam
that rose as if from a thurible. Seventeen
hands of Equus Ferus, each Eye of Brahma
like a heavenly body, tracking.

You were the trail's first snow-dust,
decay a honeyed backdrop like a painting
from Monet: magenta, saffron, burgundy.
Of woods thick with age and a teen not yet
sure-footed. No way out but through.

Between my legs, quiver of horse flesh,
the rise of rhythm a virgin blush. Cold-
breath gallop stretch around the bend—
Duck, look out for the low-hanging!—
nature bowing to its season, bats
of maple leaves diving for our faces,
snagging our manes, outgrowth leeching
our calves. The blood red of poison ivy
trampled—hooves, foot-sure, carrying me
forward. The finish line once so far ahead.

After the Final Call from the Memory Care Unit

for CM

Before
the drought ended
and the river rose too high
        to cross
and a felled black oak blocked
        our path

we used to walk the trail
        along Willow Creek
but not so far
we'd forget

then
        we could
turn back
        the skies would blue
and we could
        venture forth again

Now
        from the storm
a sandbar
        stripped of all but sun

Babysitting My Granddaughter

for Fifi

Oh, envy the sociopathic charm
of the innocent who samples
a sister's arm for its texture,
frosts her hair with mud clumps,
chews my lipstick until her mouth's
a horror flick, licks bark off a stick
like a popsicle, tastes sow bugs
out of the garden.

Body built like a Sumo wrestler—
dimpled cheeks top to bottom.
Calls to me in angel tones, but
runs until I catch her, collapses
into crying, tired clinging, for
a minute wants no mother but
her other, lets me sing her down
to sleep, the memory of distant
galaxies fading dreams.

Alejandro Waves Good-by From His Truck

My neighbor pulls out of the driveway with the last load
of furniture—dining room chairs, appliances, my almost-
new curtains and throw pillows.

I'm surprised to feel this sad. Yes, we'd looked out for
each other—their three Houdini cats, my two left thumbs—
but I've only lived here two years, and we're all busy with jobs.

Before we'd ever met, I learned she'd taught Spanish
to my granddaughter, a language perfected from her husband.
We'd exchanged phone numbers, spare keys just in case, but

now they're gone to the next town inland. It's not as if we'd
even shared a meal—oh, a beer and snacks while he hung
my new TV, took my smaller one for their bedroom in trade,

though we'd talked about a potluck sometime soon.
Her belly's just beginning to show, and they need
a second bedroom—a little girl due Christmas Day.

They'll live too far for last-minute babysitting. But
for now, he works from home. Still in this country.

Ode to My Index Finger

O, index finger. White Mountains in the distance, womb rushed
from Navy digs to Hitchcock Hospital for that epic push—yes,
all mothers are brave—to bear your wiggling digit, tiny as a ribbon.

You, milkmaid, who knew how to prime her breast as I drank,
wrap your twin around her own to dream of being grown—
that first year frost-bitten and blue as a fetus. Yet coverlet for thumb.

O, master of manipulation, now you point and the world looks,
scold and it humbles, grasp and I can hold it in my palm. Synch
to my wink with your *Come here*, baby gesture, in love with the suck.

Sense-expert, you test my baby's bottle, the cacciatore simmering
on the stove, inform me when to serve dinner, wipe what's dripped
before it hits the table. Lead the family in a *happy birthday* song.

Your love of touch, tracing the ABCs on my children's sheets
to show them how letters shape words, and at the keyboard,
how you can sound middle C. Can keep a beat, conduct a symphony!

O, Captain of my ship, assaying the winds to gauge the competition,
urging me into first place. *Let's go!* Your genius on the putting green,
tennis court, badminton. Your finger-hook with partners at the finish.

You smooth out my cursive, speed up my typing, shadow my thinking
in the air. O, gymnast, to perform without a muscle! Extend, abduct,
and flex to reach my chocolate on the shelf, dig for what I've dropped.

Now shaped the sign of Zorro, my age-scarred little hero,
your knuckle-skin layers like the rings of an ancient sequoia,
like an elephant eye winks, in the flirtation of sagging.

Sculptor

Once I took a lump of clay
and formed a hand
exactly like my left one.
Thumbs pressed the soft palette
of the palm, fingers shaped
themselves.

I fell in love
with every engraving—
age lines confused with veins,
knuckles' swollen cratered moons,
nails crooked as stigmata stains.

I uttered its name: *hand,*
placed it on my altar
next to the St. Francis prayer,
palm up, empty as a beggar's.

With Gratitude

Immeasurable gratitude to my poetry tribes for the studying, writing, and revising together, especially workshops with Joe Millar, Dorianne Laux, Cecilia Woloch, Ellen Bass, and Jeffrey Levine. Steve McDonald's dazzle of poets has been an eleven-year lifeline. And such an embarrassment of riches to share poems on-line with Seretta Martin's group, Digging In group, and my little on-line roundtable with Penny/Kate, Joni, Amanda, Carolyn, and Lisa. Thank you.

Acknowledgments

The following poems have been published in part or entirety in these journals:

"Cradlesong," *Love Is: Love Poems*, Vol. II, Johnny M. Tucker, Jr.
"Fire Only 15% Contained," *Brushfire Magazine*
"Gratitude," "Ode to What Goes Round," "Plum," *LAdige*
"How Love Shows Up," *A Walk with Nature: Poetic Encounters that Nourish the* Soul
"Ignorance as Bliss," "*Love Is*, Vol. II Anthology" ed. Johnny Tucker, Jr.
"Lament of the Golden Hawk," *San Diego Poetry Annual*
"Listening for Tchaikovsky," *Passager*, Honorable Mention
"Ode to My Index Finger," *Kestrel*
"Out the Church Window One Sunday, Swans," published as "Spotting Swans Out the Church Window," St. Marks Art Show Finalist;
"Poppy Field," *Escondido Arts Summation Anthology*
"Santa Anas: Devil Winds," *Nebo*
"Sculptor," *San Diego Arts and Poets Magazine*
"Sunrise and Dogwood: A Reconciliation," photograph by Dave Woodman, *Orchards Poetry*
"The Facts of Life," published as "Playing with Matches," *Pink Panther Magazine*
"The Golden Gate," *Evening Street Review*
"The Tor House Beach," *These Fragile Lilacs*
"Thief," *The Raven's Perch*
"To November," *Gyroscope Review*
"Umbilical Cord," *Willow Review*

O'Fallon's poems have been published in *RATTLE, MER, Tupelo Press,* etc., and four chapbooks. She has been a finalist in four book contests, and nominated for Best of the Net, 2026—a bridesmaid and not yet a bride, though she did win a short story contest. O'Fallon is a psychologist in Carlsbad.

www.ingramcontent.com/pod-product-compliance
Lightning Source LLC
Chambersburg PA
CBHW022047080426
42734CB00009B/1272